A Study Guide to Essentials of Managed Health Care

Fourth Edition

Peter R. Kongstvedt, MD, FACP

AN ASPEN PUBLICATION®
Aspen Publishers, Inc.
Gaithersburg, Maryland
2001

Library of Congress Cataloging-in-Publication Data

Orders: (800) 638-8437
Customer Service: (800) 234-1660

About Aspen Publishers • For more than 40 years, Aspen has been a leading professional
publisher in a variety of disciplines. Aspen's vast information resources are available in both print
and electronic formats. We are committed to providing the highest quality information available
in the most appropriate format for our customers. Visit Aspen's Internet site for more information
resources, directories, articles, and a searchable version of Aspen's full catalog, including the
most recent publications: **www.aspenpublishers.com**
Aspen Publishers, Inc. • The hallmark of quality in publishing
Member of the worldwide Wolters Kluwer group

Editorial Services: Ruth Bloom
Library of Congress Catalog Card Number
ISBN for *A Study Guide to Essentials of Managed Health Care, Fourth Edition*: 0-8342-1984-0
ISBN for *Essentials of Managed Health Care. Fourth Edition* and *A Study Guide to Essentials of
Managed Health Care, Fourth Edition*: 0-8342-1985-9

Printed in the United States of America

1 2 3 4 5

Contents

CHAPTER 1

An Overview of Managed Care

CHAPTER STUDY REVIEW

1. The first managed care system can be traced back to 1910 and the Western Clinic, which many cite as the first example of an HMO. One of the first health insurance plans was implemented at Baylor Hospital in Houston, Texas, in 1929. Despite the AMA's 1932 declaration of a strong stance against prepaid group practices, managed care plans continued to gain popularity. With the increase in commonality of managed care plans came increased legislative involvement. A major boost to the HMO movement was the 1973 federal HMO act. Two other major pieces of legislation affecting the managed care field were 1996's Health Insurance Portability and Accountability Act and 1997's Balanced Budget Act. Today, multistate managed care firms dominate the market, reflecting a trend toward consolidation. Most Americans with health care coverage are covered by some form of managed care plan.

2. Three areas of innovation in managed care are:
   - The collaboration of physicians and hospitals to form PHOs
   - The development of carve-outs
   - Advances made possible by computer technology

3. Managed care has matured considerably since its modest beginnings. Three aspects of the maturation of managed care are:
   - *HMO and PPO growth*: HMOs and PPOs have grown exponentially as employers have come to rely on managed care at the expense of once traditional indemnity insurance plans. Medicare and Medicaid programs have contracted increasingly with HMOs.
   - *External oversight activities*: In 1991, the National Committee for Quality Assurance (NCQA) began to accredit HMOs. Today, many employers look favorably upon, sometimes even demand, NCQA accreditation.

- *Shift in focus of cost management efforts*: Inpatient hospital utilization is still scrutinized, but more notice is being taken of ambulatory services.

4. There are three main aspects of the restructuring that has taken place in managed care.

   - *Blurred distinctions among plans*: The managed care environment is becoming increasing complicated as organizations become hybridized.
   - *Increased role of primary care physicians*: PCPs assume responsibility for the allocation of resources and have begun to rise above specialists and hospitals in their importance to managed care organizations.
   - *Consolidation among plans and providers*: Large, multistate care organizations account for the vast majority of national enrollment and there is no end in sight to the current trend toward mergers.

5. There are several key issues that will affect the future of managed care. Five of the most important issues are:

   - *Public versus private sector issues*: There has been a recent worsening of the public-private relationship for two major reasons—employees' resentment of having limited or no access to traditional indemnity programs and high cost sharing, and concern over whether managed care companies deny claims inappropriately and are otherwise overly restrictive. The government may play a greater role in managed care through increased legislation.
   - *Quality*: Some quality issues that will affect the future of HMOs include whether they will focus on maximum value rather than minimum cost, how well chronically ill patients will fare under capitated arrangements, and the role that primary care physicians will play in the care of chronically ill patients.
   - *Coverage and new technologies*: Currently, there is no procedure for deciding when a procedure is no longer considered investigational or experimental. This issue will become increasingly important with the fast pace of technology and the concurrent advances in medical treatment.
   - *Funding for the uninsured*: Managed care creates a more price-competitive environment, which reduces the financial capability of providers to care for the uninsured.
   - *Graduate medical education*: Typically, the cost of continued medical education has been addressed by higher fee-for-service costs. It remains to be seen how funding for graduate medical education will be handled in the future.

CHAPTER 2

Types of Managed Care Organizations

CHAPTER STUDY REVIEW

1. There are many types of managed care plans. Each was designed to fulfill a specific set of needs, and each has inherent strengths and weaknesses.
2. Managed care and indemnity insurance was developed to provide both cost control and freedom of choice. There are four types of managed care overlays—general utilization management, specialty utilization management, catastrophic or large-case management, and workers' compensation utilization management.
3. PPOs typically create a provider network for covered individuals by contracting directly with hospitals, physicians, and diagnostic facilities. Unlike HMOs, PPOs allow members to use non-PPO providers, but apply higher coinsurance rates or deductibles for out-of-network services. Many PPOs have utilization management programs.
4. EPOs have an organization and purpose similar to that of PPOs. Members may use participating providers for all health care services, but the plan generally does not reimburse patients for services received outside of the network. Some EPOs use primary care physicians to act as gatekeepers.
5. POS plans are hybrids of traditional HMO and PPO plans.
   - *Primary care PPOs*: Primary care physicians act as gatekeepers for referrals and institutional services. Patients have some coverage for services not authorized by the primary care physician or delivered out of network, but coverage is usually significantly lower than for in-network providers.
   - *POS HMOs*: These provide some level of indemnity-type coverage for members, who can choose which plan to use for each instance of care.
6. HMOs are organized health care systems responsible for financing and delivering a range of comprehensive health services. Some

HMOs use prepaid fixed fees and all must ensure that members have access to covered services. The differences among HMO plans pertain to relationships between the plans and participating physicians.

- *Staff model*: In this model, physicians who serve beneficiaries are employed by the HMO and are typically paid on a salary basis. These plans include physicians in common specialties to provide for members' various needs. Physicians out of network cannot participate in these plans, which provide limited choice for patients.
- *Group model*: In this model, the plan contracts with a multispecialty physician group practice and physicians are employed by the practice, not the HMO. These groups may be either captive or independent. This plan also provides a limited choice of participating physicians.
- *Network model*: In this model, the plan contracts with more than one physician group. These may be broad-based multispecialty groups or small groups, each representing different specialties. The group is responsible for providing all health care services for patients and physicians can refer to other physicians as necessary. These groups may be either closed or open panel.
- *IPA model*: In this model, the plan contracts with associations of physicians to provide services for members. This open-panel plan includes a broad range of physicians from various specialties. IPAs create organized forums for physicians to negotiate as a group with HMOs.
- *Direct contract model*: In this model, similar to the IPA model, the plan contracts directly with individual physicians. The plan recruits broad panels of community physicians, both primary care and specialists, to participate as plan providers.
- *Open access HMOs*: This model does not require a primary care service physician or gatekeeper. There may be a financial incentive for patients to see primary care physicians for referrals, but this is not required.
- *Self-insured*: In this model, the HMO receives a fixed monthly payment to cover administrative services and variable payments based on actual expenses made by the HMO for health services. There is often a settlement process at the end of specified periods in which a final payment is calculated.
- *Experience related*: In this model, the HMO receives monthly premium payments. There is often a settlement process in which the employer is credited with some or all of the actual utilization and cost of its group to reach a final premium rate. Refunds are calculated and made to the appropriate party.

CHAPTER 3

Integrated Health Care Delivery Systems

CHAPTER STUDY REVIEW

1. An IDS is created when more than one type of provider comes together in a legal structure to manage health care. The goal of an IDS is to improve efficiency in managing health care delivery.

2. There are three basic structures of an IDS:
   - Systems in which only physicians are integrated
   - Systems in which physicians are integrated with facilities
   - Systems that include insurance functions

Moving from the first to the third structure, the degree of integration and potential ability to operate in a managed care environment, the complexity of formation and operation, the required capital investment, and the surrounding political difficulties increase.

3. There are many IDS types; each has its own advantages and disadvantages.
   - *IPA*: An IPA is a legal entity comprised of independent physicians who contract with the IPA primarily to have it contract with one or more HMOs. IPAs offer a broad choice of physicians and require less capital to start than some other IDSs. However, IPAs can be unwieldy because they comprise a large body of physicians with little in common. They are also unable to leverage resources, achieve economies of scale, or significantly change behavior.
   - *PPMC*: PPMCs comprise physicians only, without the involvement of a hospital. These groups can be either for-profit, comprehensive PPMCs, or specialty PPMCs. Regardless of type, their sole purpose is to manage physicians' practices. However, PPMCs do not have a good track record, creating an atmosphere of distrust.
   - *GPWW*: A GPWW does not require the participation of a hospital and is often formed as a means for physicians to organize

without hospital support. GPWWs are owned and governed by member physicians and have the legal ability to negotiate and commit on behalf of all members. These groups lack a significant ability to manage practice behavior and they must continually seek out new sources of capital, information systems, and management expertise.

- *Consolidated medical groups*: These groups are formed when physicians combine resources to become a true medical group practice. These groups operate independently of hospitals and are able to achieve substantial economies of scale, influence physician behavior, and have the leverage to negotiate. Unfortunately, these groups often face uncontrolled overhead and have poor utilization patterns.
- *PHO*: PHOs allow a hospital and its physicians to negotiate with third-party payers; this type of IDS can be either open or closed. A drawback of the PHO model is that it is often structured loosely and fails to actually improve contracting ability.
- *MSO*: MSOs offer both a vehicle for negotiating with MCOs and additional services to support physicians' practices. These groups bind physicians closer to hospitals and can bring economies of scale and professional management to physicians' office services. However, physicians can challenge allegiances with relative ease and these groups have limited ability to enact change.
- *Foundations*: This model can be formed when a hospital creates a not-for-profit foundation and purchases physicians' practices, then places them within the foundation. Foundations are governed by boards not dominated by either the hospital or physicians. The foundation model provides a high level of structural integration and can satisfy legal constraints that prohibit hospitals from purchasing services or employing physicians. Unfortunately, there exists in the foundation model a built-in potential for conflicts between hospitals and physician groups, and foundations must continually prove that they provide a benefit for the community to retain non-for-profit status.
- *Staff models*: Staff model IDSs employ physicians directly, either by purchasing their practices or hiring them. Physicians are salaried and can enjoy incentive programs, but management sometimes treats physicians like other staff, which can cause resentment among physicians. Physicians may also have little motivation to be productive in this model.
- *Physician ownership models*: Physicians hold a significant portion, if not all, ownership in this type of model. Because of this, they have a vested interest in the system's success. Drawbacks to

this system include the high level of resources required to build and operate it, and the high buy-in cost for new physicians.

- *PSO*: PSOs are cooperative ventures of group providers who control financial arrangements and health service delivery and activity is focused on the Medicare community. The need for reserves in this model has been greatly underestimated and PSOs often do not have managerial or systems capabilities to administer the plans.

4. Virtual integration is a system under independent parties come together to behave like an IDS under managed care, yet retain their own identities and missions.

5. Four key legal issues facing an IDS are *private inurement, fraud and abuse, antitrust actions*, and *licensure provisions*.

CHAPTER 4

Elements of the Management Control and Governance Structure

CHAPTER STUDY REVIEW

1. A managed care organization's board of directors is responsible for the governance functions of the MCO. These functions include:
   - Final approval of corporate bylaws
   - General oversight of profitability or reserve status
   - Oversight and approval of significant fiscal events
   - Responsibility to protect shareholders' interest (in for-profit plans)
   - Review of reports and document signing
   - Setting and approving policy
   - Oversight of the quality management program
   - Hiring the CEO and reviewing his/her performance (in free-standing plans)

2. There are seven key management positions on the board of directors of a managed care organization. These members must act in the best interests of the organization or they could face liability issues.
   - executive director/chief operating officer
   - medical director
   - finance director
   - marketing director
   - operations director
   - director of information systems
   - corporate compliance officer

3. There are seven committees crucial to the successful operation of MCOs.
   - QM committee
   - Credentialing committee

- Medical advisory committee
- Utilization review committee
- Pharmacy and therapeutics committee
- Medical grievance review committee
- Corporate compliance committee

CHAPTER 5

Examining Common Assertions about Managed Care

CHAPTER STUDY REVIEW

1. There are many theories behind the widespread adoption of managed care. Some feel that it has been a response to the crisis of rising health care costs. Others believe that it is a result of problems with the quality of health care including underuse, overuse, misuse, and geographic variation.

2. Much of the political debate surrounding managed care has revolved around claims concerning the treatment of particular individuals' cases. Conversely, when consumers are asked directly about the quality of their personal health care, most express satisfaction.

3. Many common myths surround the issue of managed care. For each of these myths, there is either evidence that proves them false, or a lack of evidence to substantiate them.
   - *Myth*: The growth of managed care health systems has restricted choice.
   - *Myth*: Members enrolled in managed care plans received lower quality services than did those with traditional indemnity coverage.
   - *Myth*: Doctors' decisions on necessary treatment often are overruled by plans' utilization review personnel.
   - *Myth*: Physicians who participate in health plans are exposed to a greater number of medical malpractice claims because they are limited in the services they can perform.
   - *Myth*: Managed care plans do not provide coverage for the necessary duration of hospital stays.
   - *Myth*: Managed care plans avoid enrolling sick patients and achieve high quality and positive outcomes by enrolling healthier members.

- *Myth*: Managed care enrollees have more difficulty gaining access to specialty care than do patients with indemnity coverage.
- *Myth*: Women enrolled in managed care plans do not have adequate access to obstetrical and gynecological care.
- *Myth*: Health plans cause low levels of enrollment in clinical trials.
- *Myth*: Forced to see too many patients, physicians are spending less time with those patients.
- *Myth*: Health plans use "gag rules" to keep physicians from discussing with patients certain available treatment options.
- *Myth*: To generate large profits, managed care plans sacrifice quality of care.
- *Myth*: Hospitals are losing money because of increased enrollment in health plans.
- *Myth*: The increase in managed care has caused a decrease in physician profits.

4. There is a proliferation of evidence showing that managed care has helped lower health care costs and make health care more widely available.

5. Before the advent of managed care, few in the health care industry were subject to measures of quality. With the growth in managed care enrollment, most aspects of the health care delivery system are now subject to rigorous quality assessment measures.

CHAPTER 6

Primary Care in Managed Health Care Plans

CHAPTER STUDY REVIEW

1. The PCP plays a key role in the managed health care delivery system. The PCP is often the first point of contact for the patient. Acting as a gatekeeper, many PCPs refer patients to specialists when necessary.

2. Most health care systems consider three specialties primary care: *family practice*, *internal medicine*, and *pediatrics*. In some rural or underserved areas, *general practitioners* are also considered primary care physicians.

3. In creating a provider network, MCOs must take into consideration a variety of factors, including access needs and geographic requirements, needs of plan members, and variety of practitioners.

4. When developing a network, open-panel MCOs are likely to have to deal with a variety of contracting situations. Such situations include:
   - *Individual physicians*: This is the most common category in open-panel MCOs. Individual physicians contract directly with the health plan.
   - *Medical groups*: In this situation, small groups operate as cohesive units to contract MCOs.
   - *IPAs*: Independent practice associations are the original form of the open-panel plan. IPAs are legal entities that contract with physicians, then act as a negotiating body between the physicians and the MCO.
   - *IDS*: An independent delivery system can be hospital-based or physician only.
   - *FPP*: Family practice plans are organized around teaching programs and are usually found at university hospitals.

   Each situation has relative advantages and disadvantages.

5. MCOs credential physicians to ensure a level of quality and acceptability among their physicians and to protect themselves from

potential liability should a dispute arise regarding a certain provider. Credentialing is usually carried out during the recruiting process and includes significant background checks regarding issues such as prior claims, training, and status according to national data banks.

6. Networks must be actively maintained to remain positively effective. Active maintenance often includes office evaluations, medical record review, electronic connectivity review, interaction with a provider's representative, and monitoring member services complaints.

7. In any plan, there will be physicians who will not or cannot work within the system and whose style of practice is cost ineffective or of poor quality. Offending physicians may face sanctions or, in some cases, removal from the plan.

CHAPTER 7

Compensation of Primary Care Physicians in Managed Health Care

CHAPTER STUDY REVIEW

1. Managed care organizations reimburse providers through several methods, and often mix reimbursement methods rather than use one form over another.

2. *Capitation* is a system of prepayment for services on a per-member, per-month basis. Capitation rates can vary depending on such factors as age, gender, current health status, geography, and practice type. Capitation payment does *not* vary, however, based on the use of services by members.

3. A *withhold* system entails the withholding of a percentage of the primary care physician's reimbursement each month (for capitation) or each payment (for FFS). In a capitation system, the primary care physician then receives a check each month in the amount of the capitation rate minus the withhold amount. If, at the end of the year, there is money that has not been used to cover cost overruns, it is returned to the primary care physician.

4. When using capitation risk pools, services themselves may be paid for through a variety of methods, but for accounting purposes, the expense is drawn against a capitated fund or pool. The four broad categories of non-primary care risk pools are referral, hospital, ancillary services, and "other." The flow of funds and level of risk for each pool may be handled differently.

5. For purposes of year-end reconciliation, it is common for a plan to stop deducting expenses from an individual primary care physician's pool after reaching a certain threshold. This is called *stop-loss protection*, and there are two forms—costs for individual members and aggregate cost protection. The expenses incurred after the

threshold is exceeded will then be paid from an aggregate pool or a specially allocated stop-loss fund.

6. When plans track risk pools on an *individual risk* basis, physicians are at risk for their own patients' medical costs. When risk pools are tracked on a *pooled risk* basis, risk is distributed across the entire network.

7. Under *full professional risk capitation*, a primary care physician or medical group receives money for all professional services but not for hospital services. This method is generally supportable only by a large group or organized system of primary care physicians. Global capitation refers to the medical group or organized health care delivery system receiving capitation payment for all services, including institutional and other services such as pharmacy. Global capitation is supportable only by large and sophisticated medical groups, and even then, the track record of global capitation is poor in terms of financial outcomes.

8. There are many reasons for plans to capitate. Among them are that capitation puts providers at some risk or incentive for medical expenses and utilization, eliminates the FFS incentive to overuse, brings financial incentives of providers in line with those of the HMO, and makes costs more easily predictable. Providers also may benefit from capitation through the assurance of good cash flow; in some cases, profit margins also can exceed those of FFS.

9. There are also some drawbacks to capitation. There is a degree of chance involved, especially when dealing with small numbers. Practices can forget that many members of a plan are not necessarily patients, so capitation payments can seem small compared to services rendered. Finally, the financial reward is temporally remote (i.e., remote in time) from the actual medical service because the physician does not receive immediate payment.

10. In *FFS* plans, payment is distributed on the basis of expenditure of resources. Though many physicians prefer them, FFS plans are sometimes criticized because of the belief that physicians will do more if they are paid more. FFS can be either straight or performance-based.

11. In some plans, the negotiated contract provider payment rate is a percentage *discount* off the UCR or the submitted claim, whichever is lower. This is relatively rare now.

12. In a *relative value scale* (RVS) system, each procedure has associated with it a relative value. RVSs are very popular in FFS plans, but there has been a problem with the imbalance between the values of procedural and cognitive services. The *Resource Based Relative Value Scale,* developed by the Health Care Financing Administration, has been widely adopted to address this imbalance.

13. *Global fees* are single fees for all services that are delivered in an episode of care. These fees are variations on the FFS model and can be tied to performance.

14. There have been three main problems with the FFS model in managed care—churning, upcoding, and unbundling. *Churning* is when physicians perform more procedures than necessary and schedule patient visits at frequent intervals. *Upcoding* is a slow creeping upward of CPT codes that pay more. Unbundling involves charging for services previously included in a single fee without lowering, or lowering sufficiently, the original fee.

15. Federal regulations that affect reimbursement are applicable only in federally funded health plans, with Medicare and Medicaid being the primary types of plans included. These regulations include the determination of whether a physician is at *significant financial risk*, the requirement of some form of *stop-loss protection* for the protection of physicians and physician groups, *disclosure requirements* for network providers who are at financial risk, and the conduct of *customer satisfaction surveys* by MCOs.

CHAPTER **8**

Contracting and Reimbursement of Specialty Physicians

CHAPTER STUDY REVIEW

1. Depending on their qualifications, physicians can be designated as either primary or specialty care physicians.
2. The two simplest arrangements for specialist reimbursement are *straight FFS* and *discounted FFS*. Physicians can receive either straight or volume discounts. In addition, reimbursement can be based on a relative value scale or a fee allowance schedule.
3. *Performance-based FFS* can include withholds and fee adjustments similar to those discussed in chapter 7.
4. *Budgeted FFS* attempts to adjust fees based on specialty. Each specialty has a PMPM budget and actual costs for that specialty service are measured against that budget.
5. *Capitation* for specialists is a fixed payment PMPM for services. Capitation may be adjusted based on factors including age, gender, and product type.
6. *Contact capitation* begins with a capitated pool of money for each major specialty. The plan tracks each member's contact with the specialist and, after the period is over, the plan pays out the total capitated pool of money to the SCPs based on the distribution of contacts.
7. *Organized groups* of either single specialties or multiple specialties can be capitated. This is the easiest form of SCP capitation.
8. The method of capitation by *geographic distribution* involves a group being capitated for relevant specialty services in a defined portion of the medical service area, but not the entire area.
9. *Specialty IPAs* accept capitation from the HMO but usually pays FFS to participating specialists.

10. *Disease management organizations* are a variation on single-group capitation and involve capitation for specialty services to a specialty organization. That organization is then required to perform all specialty services within the covered medical area.

11. *Single-specialty management* is uncommon and involves an HMO contracting with one single entity to provide all services within a single specialty; however, the entity does not actually provide all of the services.

12. Another uncommon capitation method is *PCP choice*. In this model, each PCP selects an SCP from applicable specialties who will be used exclusively.

13. A *retainer* is yet another uncommon method of capitation in which an SCP receives a set amount each month and then reconciles with the MCO periodically based on actual utilization.

14. In an *hourly* or *salaried* arrangement, the plan pays a physician an hourly rate or salary for services performed.

15. *Case rates*, *global fees*, and *flat rates* are all single fees paid for procedures regardless of time and effort spent.

16. *Bundled case rates* are a reimbursement method that combines both the institutional and the professional charges into a single payment.

17. Sometimes plans use *periodic interim payments* (PIPs) or *cash advances*. PIPs involvement the advancement to the provider of a set amount of cash equivalent to a defined time period's expected reimbursable charges. With cash advances, the plan advances the provider a set amount of cash and then carries it as receivable on the books.

CHAPTER 9

Negotiating and Contracting with Hospitals, Institutions, and Ancillary Services

CHAPTER STUDY REVIEW

1. Developing a hospital network is a complex process involving six basic steps:
   - Selecting hospitals
   - Establishing general negotiating strategy
   - Developing data
   - Setting goals
   - Determining the responsibilities and roles of plan management
   - Determining the responsibilities and roles of hospital management

2. There are many reimbursement methods available when contracting with hospitals. In deciding which method to use, management must have the internal ability to manage these financial terms in their information systems.
   - Some plans may reimburse through either *straight charges* or a *straight discount on charges*. With a straight discount, the hospital submits its claim and the plan discounts it by an agreed-upon percentage.
   - A *sliding scale discount* is a percentage discount that is reflective of the total volume of admissions and outpatient procedures.
   - A negotiated *per diem* is a single charge for a day in the hospital regardless of any actual charges or costs incurred. A *sliding scale per diem* is based on total volume.
   - Sometimes, per diem reimbursement is combined with *differential by day in hospital*, in which the first day is paid at a higher rate.

- A common reimbursement method is by *DRGs,* in which the plan negotiates a payment mechanism for DRGs on the basis of Medicare or state-regulated rates.
- *Service-related case rates* are similar to DRGs, and in this case, the hospital receives a flat per-admission reimbursement for the type of service for which the patient is admitted.
- *Case rates* and *package pricing* are set rates for certain categories of procedures.
- *Capitation* is the reimbursement of the hospital on a PMPM basis. *Percentage of revenue*, unlike capitation, may vary with the premium rate charged and the actual revenue yield.
- *Contact capitation* involves reimbursement in which the capitation is tied to the percentage of admissions to a hospital, with some adjustments for type of service provided.
- *Bed leasing* is a rare practice and entails the plan actually leasing beds from an institution, regardless of whether those beds are used or not.
- *PIPs* and *cash advances* are also rare. Cash advances are replenished if they get below a certain amount and provide hospitals with positive cash flow.
- Capitation is one form of *performance-based reimbursement.* Other forms include *penalties*, *withholds*, and *service and quality incentives.*

3. Reimbursement for outpatient procedures does not necessarily mirror that for inpatient services, but the two do have some methods in common.
   - Providers may be reimbursed through *straight* or *sliding scale discounts on charges.*
   - Plans may negotiate *package pricing* or *bundled charges* for outpatient procedures.
   - Ambulatory visits may be reimbursed through *APGs* and *APCs*, which are similar to DRGs for inpatient services.

4. *Ancillary services* are those that are provided as an adjunct to basic primary or specialty services. They include almost everything other than institutional services. Pharmacy services are included in ancillary services.

5. Many ancillary services are carved out of the main medical delivery system and the risk is transferred to another organization. These organizations can achieve economies of scale and manage overall cost and quality.

6. HMO plans that have absolute limitations on benefits provided for ancillary services often use capitation. Some plans, such as a POS, may use capitation only for in-network charges and pay out-of-network charges with regular fee allowances.

CHAPTER 10

Care Management and Clinical Integration Components

CHAPTER STUDY REVIEW

1. The primary objective of advanced care management is to ensure that each enrollee receives the appropriate level of care (including preventive services) at the lowest cost, with optimal outcomes. Advanced care management involves the evaluation of care in all settings against a more comprehensive set of criteria and within more aggressive time frames.

2. Advanced care management is a comprehensive, integrated program that allows an organization to effectively assess and manage the clinical performance of its providers and the health status of the insured population.

3. Care management models move away from typical insurance-focused programs, instead evolving into care delivery, and eventually continuum of care, models. In such models, care management drives patient care.

4. To convert program elements into an integrated care management system, organizations must invest in the core program elements, develop the supporting infrastructure, and determine the appropriate integration model.

5. Organizational integration is driven by the theory that controlling all the inputs of the health care process can result in improved quality and service, lower cost structure, and the critical mass necessary to become a dominant player in the market.

6. There are eight key characteristics of advanced care management.
   - Multidisciplinary teams drive the development and ongoing operation of the care management system.
   - Communication and documentation are enhanced throughout the system.

- Patient care and services across the different settings and departments are well coordinated.
- Processes are streamlined and resources are effectively managed to improve service and reduce costs.
- There is a marked reduction in the duplication of clinical and administrative efforts.
- Services are redesigned to allow departments and operating units to share resources, as appropriate.
- Internal and external customer satisfaction improves throughout the health system.
- Within the health care organization, care management is functionally and structurally situated as a core business.

7. In an advanced care management system, physicians act as partners with the health system. They remain the primary providers of patient care services and manage the overall health of their patients.

8. The development of an advanced care management system typically includes four phases:
   - Elaboration of mission and vision, current state assessment
   - Future state design, including the benchmarking of leading practices
   - Construction of the model and long-term plan
   - Staged implementation

CHAPTER 11

Managing Basic Medical-Surgical Utilization

CHAPTER STUDY REVIEW

1. One of the principal objectives of utilization management is the reduction of practice variation by establishing parameters for cost-effective use of health care resources. The techniques used to manage utilization serve to contain cost while ensuring the provision of appropriate care.
2. MCOs have enjoyed a high rate of return on their investment in utilization management activities in the form of lower health care costs.
3. Demand management is a set of activities designed to reduce the overall requirement for health care services by members. These activities can include:
   - *Nurse advice lines*: These provide members with access to advice on medical conditions, the need for medical care, health promotion and preventive care, and similar health-related activities.
   - *Self-care and medical consumerism programs*: This entails the provision of information to members to enable them to provide care for themselves or better evaluate when they need to seek care from a professional.
   - *Shared decision-making programs*: These programs involve making patients active participants in choosing their courses of care.
   - *Medical informatics*: This broad term applies to the use of information technology in the management of health care delivery.
   - *Preventive services and health risk appraisals*: Common preventive services include immunizations, mammograms, routine physical examinations and health assessment, and counseling regarding behaviors that members can undertake to lower their

risk of ill health. The health risk appraisal is a tool to elicit information from a member regarding certain activities and behaviors that can influence health status.

4. There are two primary means of measuring utilization—*physician utilization data* and *hospital utilization data*. With physician utilization data, there is no set standard for reporting data on referral utilization, and counting only the initial referral or authorization may result in missing a large portion of actual utilization. Regarding hospital utilization data, a choice must be made as to what will be measured and that measurement must be defined precisely. Two ways in which hospital utilization data may vary are by geography and by practice.

5. The PCP plays a key role in utilization management. In this type of authorization system, a member may visit a PCP without any barriers to access, but to see a specialist, the member must obtain authorization from the PCP. If the member does not obtain authorization, the plan may not pay for unauthorized services (HMO plans) or may offer a lower level of payment (POS plans).

6. Some systems allow only one visit per authorization. These systems, called *single-visit authorization* systems, provide the highest degree of utilization management.

7. In certain circumstances—usually those in which a member has a chronic disease—it is better for a specialist to act as PCP.

8. Three common methods for managing utilization are:
   - *Prospective review*: The review of cases before they happen.
   - *Concurrent review*: The review of cases while they are active.
   - *Retrospective review*: The review of cases after they are finished.

CHAPTER 12

Clinical Services Requiring Authorization

CHAPTER STUDY REVIEW

1. Authorization systems are a definitive element of managed health care systems, and there are several reasons for their use. Authorization systems allow the medical management function of a plan to review a case for medical necessity, channel care to the most appropriate function, provide timely information to the concurrent utilization review system and to large case management, and help finance to estimate the accruals for each month's medical expenditures.

2. Authorization systems have set definitions regarding which services require authorization and which do not. The tighter the authorization system, the greater the plan's ability to manage utilization.

3. No managed care systems require authorization for primary care services, only for nonprimary services.

4. Plans also designate who can authorize services; this designation varies by plan type and the degree to which it is medically managed.

5. Authorizations can be classified into six categories:
   - *Prospective*: This is sometimes called "precertification" because authorization is issued before service is rendered.
   - *Concurrent*: Authorization is generated at the time of service.
   - *Retrospective*: Authorization is granted after service is performed.
   - *Pended (for review)*: A period of time when it is not known whether an authorization will be issued because of a question regarding coverage for a service, medical necessity, coordination of benefits, correction of claims errors or duplicate claims, or other reasons requiring additional investigation.
   - *Denial*: It is certain that authorization is denied and no payment is forthcoming.

- *Subauthorization*: This is a special category that allows one authorization to "hitchhike" with another.

6. The three main methods of authorization issuance are *paper-based authorization systems*, *telephone-based authorization systems*, and *electronic authorization systems*.

7. HIPAA will mandate the ANSI X 12N standards including those for referral authorization, for electronic transmissions as of November 2002.

CHAPTER 13

Case Managed and Managed Care

CHAPTER STUDY REVIEW

1. Case management is an important component of the managed care strategy. Case managers work in the provider sector in practice settings, as well as in the payer sector, representing employers through third-party administrators and self-administered programs, employed within health maintenance programs or by major insurance carriers.
2. Case managers fill six main roles:
   - Coordinators of care
   - Catalysts
   - Problem solvers
   - Facilitators
   - Impartial advocates
   - Educators
3. Case managers take part in a variety of activities including medical, financial, behavioral or motivational, and vocational activities.
4. The case management process can, and often does, involve 14 basic elements:
   - Gathering and assessing information
   - Making an initial assessment
   - Talking with the referral source
   - Talking with the patient
   - Talking with the patient's family
   - Talking with the treating physicians
   - Being involved in independent medical or second opinion exams
   - Talking with service and equipment providers
   - Talking with community resources
   - Planning
   - Reporting
   - Obtaining approval from the payer

- Coordinating and monitoring
- Evaluating the plan

5. Case managers are not used for all cases, but instead for complex cases, usually involving high-risk members.

6. There are many red flags that indicate that a case should be closely managed. Such indicators include a high frequency of admissions in a short time, an unusually lengthy hospital stay, extension of treatment, catastrophic illness, multiple hospitalizations, multiple physicians, and expenses incurred beyond a certain threshold.

7. Case management greatly benefits claims management. Case managers help to identify the claimants responsible for generating the majority of claims, educate claims administrators regarding medical issues, help manage benefit dollars, help patients get approval in a timely fashion, and help speed the claims administration process.

8. Case management can also include wellness programs, 24-hour coverage programs, and disease management programs.

CHAPTER 14

Fundamentals and Core Competencies of Disease Management

CHAPTER STUDY REVIEW

1. The goal of disease management is to reduce the frequency and severity of exacerbations of a chronic illness so that readmission costs are reduced.
2. In the past, MCOs have struggled to improve their medical loss ratios. As a result, they have discovered that secondary and tertiary prevention efforts can enact greater savings than primary efforts alone.
3. There are nine general characteristics specific to disease management:
   - Physicians are members of a caregiving team, not the center of caregiving.
   - Nonphysician practitioners deliver most of the care.
   - Most care is delivered in an ambulatory care setting rather than an inpatient setting.
   - Guidelines and outcomes are more condition specific than body specific.
   - Care is delivered more often over the telephone and Internet than in person.
   - Organizations focus more on education and less on invasive medical procedures.
   - Conditions that show modifiable variability in resource use or morbidity are preferred.
   - Data must be collected from all sites of care on an annual basis.
   - In most environments, fee-for-service physicians and hospitals are not financially rewarded for good disease management.
4. The convergence of health care and the Internet has enhanced disease management and increasingly sophisticated applications for

health care management via the Internet are being developed to correct the inefficiencies and deficiencies of the current model.

5. Several advantages of Internet use are its unique ability to accomplish mass customization, transfer knowledge at a negligible cost to users, and take advantage of continuous function that can reduce the time from symptom change to treatment change.

6. Six determinants of a patient's risk level are:
   - How well the patient understands the disease
   - How well the patient learns
   - How well the patient cooperates with the provider
   - The severity of illness measures
   - The patient's resource use patterns
   - The modifiability of the course of the disease

CHAPTER 15

Prescription Drug Benefits in Managed Care

CHAPTER STUDY REVIEW

1. By the early 1980s, most large HMOs had implemented strategies to contain physician and hospital costs. HMOs then decided to turn their attention to developing strategies to contain pharmacy costs.
2. There are two primary factors responsible for pharmacy cost increases—drug price inflation and an increase in the rate of drug use.
3. Managed care organizations are faced with the challenge of providing affordable access to required medications at a cost acceptable to pharmacy-benefit purchasers. Many consumers have identified access to affordable medication as the most important aspect of their health care.
4. Managed care attempts to influence supply and demand. Supply-side contracts between MCOs and pharmaceutical manufacturers and dispensing pharmacies provide discounts on drug ingredient costs and dispensing fees. On the demand side, members must pay prescription copayments or coinsurance to access pharmacy services. Some MCOS also share financial risk of pharmacy benefits with physicians.
5. Like most modern businesses, pharmacies and pharmacy benefits' administrators rely on various data and information systems.
   - *Pharmacy claims adjudication systems*: 95 percent of prescription claims can be processed electronically online, often in real time.
   - *Online transaction processing systems*: These are MCO management information systems that store prescription records, member medical histories and utilization patterns, provider activities, claims administration, and financial records.
   - *Pharmacy and medical claims integration*: Medical and pharmacy databases are linked through common shared dimensions, including identifiers for member, physician, and employer group.

- *Electronic data interchange and electronic commerce*: Successful installation of SCRIPT application will help increase formulary conformance, adherence to drug guidelines, and increase pharmaceutical manufacturer contract performance.
- *Electronic prescribing*: This is an electronic data interchange application that provides physician connectivity with the pharmacy to allow online transmission of prescription orders.
- *Pharmacy services and health telematics*: These systems use information technology and enlightened health care practitioners to advance health care promotion and outcomes.
- *Internet patient marketing*: This is a version of direct-to-consumer marketing that takes place on the Internet and is aimed at influencing patient behavior.

6. Pharmacy benefit management companies (PBMs) are specialized business entities established to provide a broad spectrum of outsourced pharmacy benefit management services for the private and public payer-customers on a stand-alone or carve-out basis.

7. There are several reasons for MCOs to use PBMs. These include:
   - Lower developmental and operational program costs
   - Reduced development time
   - A breadth of flexible data processing services
   - Increased clinical and patient care services

8. There are three primary channels to distribute pharmaceuticals—owned, in-house pharmacies within health plan medical centers; independent and chain community retail pharmacies; and mail service and Internet pharmacies.

9. Well-designed, thorough auditing systems, combined with effective member and provider education program, can help minimize the amount of fraud and abuse common to large pharmacy provider networks.

10. A drug formulary is a preferred list of medications developed by the health plan or PBM to guide physician prescribing and pharmacy dispensing. Formularies are used as a means of controlling inventory and promoting the use of the most cost-effective products. A formulary system is the method and processes used that continually update the formulary's content of prescription medications.

11. Managed care members are usually required by contract to pay a copayment for each prescription they obtain. There are three basic reasons for this:
    - This method involves the patient as a financial risk-sharing partner.
    - Copayments should influence the patient's behavior, encouraging the patient to select a lower copayment drug that has a lower cost to the HMO or PBM.

- This method introduces a hesitation factor designed to discourage unnecessary or trivial use of prescription drugs.

12. Drug utilization review is a common clinical pharmacy procedure that involves a pharmacist's thorough review of patient drug history records to determine whether a patient's drug use or a physician's drug prescribing requires intervention. Drug utilization review helps to ensure appropriate drug therapy.

CHAPTER 16

Managed Behavioral Health Care and Chemical Dependency Services

CHAPTER STUDY REVIEW

1. Behavioral health (BH) problems tend to be chronic and recurrent in nature, and BH diagnostic categories do not follow by-the-book utilization management because there are no standard lengths of stay and treatment protocols for specified diagnoses. Managing BH is often much more complicated than managing medical-surgical care.

2. BH commonly includes mental health, substance abuse or chemical dependency, and serious mental illness or brain disorders.

3. Although general health care is technology intensive, BH care is more labor intensive (with the exception of psychopharmacology).

4. There are seven primary goals of BH treatment:
   - To improve the BH status of a defined population
   - To improve the clinical status of a population in terms of symptomatic distress levels
   - To improve life functioning in several areas
   - To reduce suicide rates
   - To reduce homicide rates
   - To reduce substance abuse-related impairments
   - To reduce mortality and morbidity from accidents related to substance abuse or mental disorders

5. There are four key principles fundamental to clinical treatment in specialized managed BH care.
   - *Alternatives to psychiatric hospitalization*: Plans often use plans involving partial hospitalization.
   - *Alternatives to restrictive treatment for substance abuse*: Some patients may benefit from outpatient rather than inpatient treatment programs.

- *Goal-directed psychotherapy*: These systems emphasize therapy designed to be brief and time limited.
- *Crisis intervention*: This is a key service in the overall service offering. Crisis intervention is an effective way to diminish the incidence of future crises and can reduce substantially the inappropriate use of psychiatric care.

6. Specialized BH programs make use of both utilization review and case management in managing utilization.

7. There are three potential gatekeepers in managed BH care systems who may refer a patient for BH care.
   - An employee assistance program
   - A primary care physician
   - A mental health or substance abuse care manager and assessor

8. Integrated delivery systems are essential to managed BH care because the nature of psychiatric and addiction disorders and the secondary disabilities that manifest as a result of the severity and persistence of these disorders. A broad range of treatment options and interventions must be simultaneously available in order to respond to the unique demands of managed BH care.

9. Managed BH programs make use of quality management activities to prevent or correct quality problems. Core activities focus on the qualifications and behavior of case managers and providers and sometimes on the treatment results achieved by providers.

CHAPTER 17

Quality Management in Managed Care

CHAPTER STUDY REVIEW

1. There are five traditional criteria for health care quality assessment.
   - *Structural measures* of health care performance are focused on the context in which care and services are provided.
   - *Process-of-care measures* evaluate the way in which care is provided.
   - Most *outcomes measurements* focus on measurements of infection rates, morbidity, and mortality.
   - *Peer review* centers on a comparison of an individual provider's practice either with practice by the provider's peers or with an acceptable standard of care.
   - *Appropriateness evaluation* includes a review of the extent to which the MCO provides timely, necessary care at the right level of service.
2. External customers of MCOs include members or benefactors and purchasers. The departments and services in the MCOs are the internal customers.
3. Customers want to know whether an MCO meets their expectations. In addition, purchasers and members value access and appropriateness. Also of import to purchasers are value assessments of disease screening activities, service quality, and encounter outcomes. In addition, to maintain health and functional capacity, MCOs must support prevention of illness and management of health status. There are three key steps in identifying processes and outcomes that meet customer need:
   - *Treating disease*
   - *Managing health*
   - *Ensuring service quality*
4. A key step in the performance improvement process is to assess plan performance compared with professional or "best-of-class" stan-

dards. This includes appropriateness evaluation, peer review, benchmarking, and outcomes assessment.

5. Legislators and politicians are acting increasingly as advocates for consumers in demanding freedom of choice and access to treatment. As consumerism in managed health care rises, it will be increasingly necessary for MCOs to identify and satisfy consumer needs and demands.

CHAPTER 18

Using Data and Provider Profiling in Medical Management

CHAPTER STUDY REVIEW

1. Data and information are powerful tools that enable medical managers to carry out necessary functions. Managers' abilities to use data and information intelligently to manage health care delivery systems is a key factor in distinguishing plans that excel.

2. There are several key requirements that make data more useful to end users.
   - Users must be able to access usable data as directly as possible.
   - Access must be as timely and easy to use as possible.
   - Managers should consider flexibility with data.

3. Managers must be able to use system data with other tools. That is, they should be able to obtain data from the system that can be used with other analytic tools and be able to download or export data into other programs.

4. It should be decided in advance which reports will be required on a routine basis and which will be ordered on an ad hoc basis.

5. There are several requirements for useful data:
   - Data must be clean.
   - Data must be valid.
   - Data must be of an appropriate sample size.
   - Data must encompass an adequate time period.
   - Data from multiple sources should be linked appropriately.
   - Data must be consistent and mean the same thing from provider to provider.

6. The HIPAA created a stringent minimum set of privacy and security standards for protecting the confidentiality of patient information. The implementing regulations for electronic business transactions also include detailed technical specifications based on ANSI X 12N transaction standards.

7. Data elements can be taken from many sources. Some of the most common sources are claims-based data, encounter-based data, medical records-based data, member questionnaires, and publicly available hospital data.

8. Data can be used to generate many types of reports. Some general reports include:
   - *Plan average*: This report looks at the average performance of the entire plan.
   - *Individual physician*: As its name suggests, this report includes profiles of individual physicians.
   - *Premium source group*: This report tracks utilization and other data by enrolled groups.
   - *Hospital reports*: Daily logs serve as utilization management tools and monthly summaries are used to identify patterns of overall management.
   - *Outpatient utilization*: These reports are usually produced monthly and help to manage referral and outpatient utilization.
   - *Open-access plans*: These plans are more difficult to manage because they do not use a primary care gatekeeper model. Reports focus on those areas under the control of the specialist, as well as primary care.

9. When using provider profiles to effect quality improvement, the two types of variables that can be profiled are those that relate to costs and those that have a closer relationship to the traditional understanding of quality. Customers and users of provider profiles include managed care organizations, enrollees, employers, and providers.

10. Provider profiles are compared to two sets of norms—internal and comparative. Internal norms are used only if the plan has enough enrollees or patients and comparative norms use external data.

11. The issues of case mix and severity are common issues of contention when profiling providers. The traditional methods that served as a proxy for severity and case-mix adjustments are the variables of age and sex. Regardless of the many other variables that can effect utilization, case-mix adjustments for quality improvement or utilization management represent only the first step in the quality improvement process.

12. Many MCOs purchase or license services from outside vendors or profiling systems. There are three basic types of products:
   - Database or database management tolls that allow the collection of information and reporting of that information in useful formats.
   - Tools that interface with data management and provide "clinical logic."
   - Risk adjustment systems that provide the user with the assurance that data are being compared with like data.

CHAPTER 19

Physician Behavior Change in Managed Health Care

CHAPTER STUDY REVIEW

1. Physicians work in a complex and emotionally charged atmosphere in which practice behavior change must occur. There are eight main aspects of practice behavior.

   - *Environment*: Physicians face a continually changing practice environment affected by pressures that drive up medical costs, shifting population demographics, advances in medical interventions, changes in drug costs, shifts of focus to quality and outcomes plus cost, and an increased focus on overall practice behavior.

   - *Medical education*: Formal medical education affects physicians' attitudes toward managed care, often negatively. In addition, formal education addresses clinical approaches to patient care, has a socializing effect, and increases knowledge and understanding of medical care.

   - *Autonomy and control needs*: There is often a conflict between a physician's need for autonomy and the controlling aspect of managed care.

   - *Role conflict*: Physicians are often viewed as patients' advocates, but are faced with the challenge of rationing care. Such situations can cause feelings of conflict between the physician's duties to a patient and to the managed care plan.

   - *Understanding of the plan*: Some conflict may result from a physician's lack of understanding of the insurance function of the plan.

   - *Bad habits*: Physicians may apply bad habits to clinical practice. These bad habits are often not cost-effective and are difficult to change.

- *Poor understanding of economics*: Physicians and business administrators may not understand the economics of the plan. To understand the economics of the plan, physicians need continual communication, re-education, and accurate and timely feedback.
- *Poor differentiation among competing plans*: The apparent similarity of competing plans can be a source of confusion for physicians. This problem is exacerbated when patients switch to different plans. To combat this confusion, plans must increase communication with physicians and staff.

2. Some general approaches to changing physician behavior include clearly translating goals and objectives into terms meaningful to physicians to increase understanding and buy-in, implementing a reward or positive feedback system, and active and ongoing involvement with participating physicians.

3. There are several programmatic approaches that can positively influence physician behavior. One such approach is a system of formal CME; however, evidence of effectiveness of using CME for this purpose is lacking. Another method is the regular provision of accurate data and feedback; however, the utility of feedback in the absence of other change management activities is mixed. Practice guidelines may be used to guide physicians in the care of patients with defined diseases or symptoms; however, gaining compliance with practice guidelines or protocols is best focused on a small number of important clinical conditions. Small group programs can also influence physician behavior; these programs involve educating physicians in highly interactive, small group settings and have proven to be quite effective. Last, using respected physician leaders in one-on-one discussions with physicians as necessary (so-called "clinical detailing") has been shown to be highly effective but resource intensive.

4. General and programmatic approaches may work to positively influence the behavior of most physicians, but they will not work for all. Broad, programmatic approaches should not be instituted for purposes of addressing behavior issues that are confined to a small number of physicians. By doing so, unnecessary and burdensome requirements are placed on the entire network for no good purpose. In the case of individual physicians who exhibit poor practice behavior that requires change, it then becomes necessary to address issues of noncompliance through a stepwise approach. This approach begins with a simple collegial discussion then, as needed, may move to attempts at persuasion, and the firm direction of plan policies, procedures, and requirements.

5. If the stepwise approach proves unsuccessful, physician behavior should be addressed with increasing serious interventions from "ticketing," to a disciplinary letter, to formal sanctioning, and finally to termination of the physician's contract. Medical managers must be aware of applicable federal and state laws and regulations regarding termination of physicians from a network, and comply as appropriate.

CHAPTER 20

Information Systems in Managed Health Care Plans

CHAPTER STUDY REVIEW

1. The quality of a health plan's information systems correlates directly to its ability to be competitive in the health care marketplace.
2. Managed care organizations rely on technology and information systems to provide services. These information systems are centered on four operational competencies:
   - *Claim payment*: Claim processing and payment is at the core of all managed care systems.
   - *Enrollment*: Enrollment modules track new records and updates to existing records, as well as terminations. Systems tracks provider, employer group, and member enrollment.
   - *Premium billing*: This is the primary source of income for health plans.
   - *Provider reimbursement*: This is the key output for claims processing. Information systems support several methods of reimbursement including capitation, fee-for-service, withholds, or a combination of these.
3. There are several advantages of EDI. EDI assists with automation, lowers the administrative ratio, and allows the plan to streamline its service levels for claim payment and enrollment. EDI also eliminates manual entry for claims, which increases greatly the accuracy with which claims information is entered and lessens the need for hired staff. Finally, using EDI enables faster payment of providers as well as the development of proprietary interfaces to support the unique needs of the plan's customers.
4. HIPAA sets forth several provisions to protect confidentiality and privacy. HIPAA focuses on requirements for the maintenance of the physical security of health information and outlines standards for maintaining reasonable and appropriate administrative, technical, and physical safeguards. The Act prohibits wrongful disclosures of

individually identifiable health information, as well as the sale of patient-identifiable data for marketing or sales purposes.

5. There are four main privacy-related corporate compliance functions required under HIPAA:

- The designation of a privacy official responsible for the development and implementation of privacy policies and procedures
- Training of all members of the workforce who obtain protected health information
- Administrative, technical, and physical safeguards to protect the privacy of protected health information
- Detailed specifications of what must be documented to ensure compliance

There are three additional administrative compliance requirements under HIPAA:

- Compliance with standardized codes sets
- Compliance with standardized electronic transaction sets
- Compliance with standardized identifiers

6. There are many expanded or new services (value added services) that health plans can offer to their customers.

- *Internet technology services*: The plan can either allow direct access to the individual health plan systems or develop an interface system for predetermined functions such as enrollment.
- *Customer services*: In order to have NCQA accreditation, plans must tracks contacts, issues, resolution, and turnaround times and must use this contact and resolution data.
- *Medical management information systems*: Proactive and intensive medical or care management represents a plan's greatest opportunity to improve health care use, quality, and cost. Information systems help with case, referral, authorization, and disease management.
- *Decision support services*: The provision of timely, complete information to the provider can aid the delivery of managed care and member health.
- *Data sets, enhancers, data warehouses, and reporting*: Health plans can leverage data sets for analytical purposes and create a continuum of care by using the information captured within its systems. Health plans can then purchase or develop data enhancers that add new characteristics to the claims records. This serves to aid the analytical process. A data warehouse can be leveraged to produce reports for use by the health plan, provider, and employer.

- ***HEDIS***: HEDIS was the NCQA's response to employer groups who wanted to understand the value of their health care dollars. It is used by public purchasers, regulators, and consumers to understand and rate a health plan's overall value and quality. HEDIS is updated on a regular basis to reflect advances in the industry.

CHAPTER 21

Claims and Benefits Administration

CHAPTER STUDY REVIEW

1. In managed care organizations, more than three-quarters of all premium dollars are paid out in capitation and claims payments. The claims function of an organization is dependent on many other functions and departments within the MCO.

2. The claims department acts as the middleman between internal and external groups and is the last point in the organization's activity flow other than the banking function of funds transfer between the plan and the provider (or member).

3. There are five basic purposes for the claims and benefits administration department.

   - *Plan contract administration*: The department meets relevant contractual obligations to groups, members, and providers.

   - *Benefits administration*: The department ensures coverage for the defined benefits population.

   - *Medical management policy administration*: The department establishes services and procedures that require prior approval with MCO medical staff and coordinates with medical management to determine the types of cases that must receive clinical review for coverage determination as well as those that can be processed by claims staff using specific guidelines and procedures. Many aspects of medical policy administration are routinely automated; e.g., payment policies for a second surgeon, service-diagnosis matching.

   - *Member and provider service*: This is better known as customer service. Benefits and claims administration is the point at which the MCO can demonstrate its ability to deliver on its service promise.

- *Liability protection*: The department holds itself out for coverage of defined benefits in the types, quantities, time frames, and reimbursement amounts specified.
4. The claims and benefits administration department provides the MCO with four key opportunities. These are:
   - To provide excellent customer service to providers and members;
   - To establish and maintain effective relationships with corporate colleagues;
   - To identify weak spots in both precedent and subsequent processes; and
   - To observe any extant inconsistencies between documents and/ or loopholes in particular documents.
5. The claims department may be structured in many ways depending on several factors including the size of the plan and possible MIS deficiencies. The main element in structuring an effective workflow is the determination of communication requirements among and between units and the design of efficient methods for claims to cross-organizational boundaries.
6. There are several elements that contribute to the effectiveness of claims operations management.
   - *Inventory control*: Claims and benefits administration must work to control its inventory as a means of supporting corporate management of assets and liabilities. The elements of inventory control are a definition of inventory, the definition of an acceptable level of inventory, a method of evaluating current inventory, a method of controlling inventory, and a method of reporting on inventory.
   - *Pended claims management*: This often accounts for the largest part of a claims and benefits administration's problem cases. The volume of these claims is linked directly to the accuracy and completeness of preceding functions such as enrollment and utilization management. Management of these claims depends on careful planning for and understanding of the rules that will be applied to the claims adjudication process manually, the predetermination of guidelines and procedures for addressing these situations, and a satisfactory mechanism for tracking and monitoring.
   - *Task allocation and work distribution*: Claims can be categorized by either type or complexity, and employees' responsibilities can be divided by type of claim. The claims department not only pays claims, but also records all use rendered to eligible members. The control of separate tasks can be controlled by task, initiating events, interim milestones achievable through the completion of measurable tasks, and recognizable goals.

- *Work flow*: The design of work flow takes into consideration the various processing points for claims from receipt by the organization through adjudication to final disposition and storage. This design must combine inventory control functions with processing functions to make claims processing as efficient as possible.
- *Electronic claims submission*: The electronic submission of claims helps to reduce claims data entry tasks. Some plans can resolve claims in real time with online edits, and these plans must maintain and manage two operational flows—one for manual entry data claims processed to completion online and one for batch review and resolution of the previous day's pend report based on manual claims pended and electronic claims that did not process.

7. The largest part of claims and benefits administration is to process claims accurately and on time. Productivity management includes the establishment of goals, the observation of the current time frames and processes for producing, and the monitoring of performance in relation to productivity goals.

8. Turn around time (TAT) is the measure—expressed in days—of the claims and benefits administration department's responsiveness to both provider and member clients. The TAT measures time frames for all points between the claim's date of receipt and date of final disposition. TAT is a number that may be defined inconsistently from one plan to another, but should refer to when the plan *receives* the claim (not the date of service, nor the day the plan begins to adjudicate the claim) and when the plan finalized disposition (not necessarily when the claim is closed out, but rather when the funds transfer or check is actually remitted).

9. The staff of the claims and benefits administration department must include experienced claims examiners. In addition, staff must receive appropriate orientation and classroom training, should be subject to self-assessment, and should participate in appropriate cross-training and job enrichment programs.

10. Quality is the overall measure of the accuracy and completeness of the product of the claims and benefits administration process. To ensure quality, a set of standards must be developed. These standards should address overall, payment, and financial accuracy. Auditing criteria should then be established and the process should be discussed with departmental staff. Finally, a claims QA process and a process for reporting results should be established.

11. Policies and procedures are the foundation of the claims and benefits administration department. Administrative policies and procedures serve to instruct staff on processes internal to the department. Coordinative policies and procedures address ways in which claims

staff interact with other departments and functions to acquire information or decisions necessary to complete claims processing. Finally, medical-operational policies and procedures include internal guidelines and instructions used in the MCO's authorization of care and the adjudication of associated claims.

12. There are several business functions included in the claims process including
    - determination of plan liability;
    - administration of benefits;
    - pricing, or determination of the contractual reimbursement amount, member cost sharing, and OPL;
    - customer service;
    - clinical or clerical and financial adjustments;
    - management reporting; and
    - claims business function reporting.

13. There are many problems common to claims and benefits administration. These include:
    - Claims backlogs
    - Inadequate front-end control
    - Inadequate pended claims management
    - Outdated departmental structure or task allocation
    - Problems with the integrity of supporting data files
    - Problems with the configuration of benefits
    - Informal benefits interpretation
    - A clash between utilization and claims management

CHAPTER 22

Member Services and Consumer Affairs

CHAPTER STUDY REVIEW

1. The member services and consumer affairs department fill several key functions:
   - To help members understand how to use the plan
   - To help resolve members' problems and/or questions
   - To monitor and track the nature of member contacts
   - To allow members to express dissatisfaction with their care
   - To help members seek review of claims that have been denied or covered at a lower than expected level of benefits
   - To manage members' problems with payments
   - To help address routine business issues
2. Though exact training and staffing requirements vary by plan, all plans should include new employee training processes, staffing ratios dependent on plan complexity, growth rate, and size, and some form of automated support.
3. Member services can be accessed by three main modes of communication—mail and paper-based, telephone, and electronic communication. For each mode, there should be performance criteria and evaluation systems.
4. The member services department helps members use the plan and disseminates information to the membership. The department provides information on such plan aspects as hours of availability and the availability of non-English communications. The department also helps with claims issues including appeals and denials of payment, enrollment and the issuance of identification cards, and the selection of primary care physicians and access to the network.
5. The member services department can take a proactive stance through outreach programs, including contacting members to discuss the way the plan works, mailing information packs to members, and establishing telephone-based information systems.

6. Collection, collation, and analysis of data also fall under the purview of the member services department. Member satisfaction data can be garnered through surveys and direct mail campaigns. Trends analysis can help identify random versus widespread problems. Appropriate data are usually obtained through automated tracking systems.

7. Proactive approaches to member services include the implementation of member education programs, the solicitation of member suggestions and recommendations, and the provision of a wide variety of special services, affiliations, and health promotion activities.

8. The member services department also handles member complaints and grievances. Complaints are episodes of dissatisfaction by the member with the plan, whereas grievances are formal complaints demanding resolution by the plan.

CHAPTER 23

Sales and Marketing in Managed Health Care Plans: The Process of Distribution

CHAPTER STUDY REVIEW

1. MCOs deliver a complex product of a delivery system that, ideally, offers consumers high-quality medical services at a price that is affordable. There are many challenges posed to the delivery of such a product including:

   - *Meeting choice-based competition*: Today's market includes an increasing focus on customer choice, which has become a significant basis for MCO competition.
   - *Increasing access to information*: To keep pace with technology and resultant consumer demands, MCOs must develop Internet and e-commerce technology, yet still remain within the boundaries set forth by HIPAA security and privacy requirements.
   - *Increased focus on quality issues*: MCOs now need to obtain external validation from organizations like the NCQA and the Joint Commission.
   - *The importance of strategic goals*: There is an increased need for the definition and maintenance of a primary strategic focus.
   - *Regulatory pressures*: The managed care industry is under increased scrutiny by consumers, consumer advocates, and politicians.
   - *Consolidation*: MCO mergers are taking place in part to extend an organization's geographic reach, gain economies of scale, and increase competitiveness in certain areas.
   - *Increasing medical costs*: MCOs are continually pressured to keep costs down, yet many of the costs of providing care are increasing.

2. Many employers now use brokers or consultants to help assist in the decision-making process of selecting a health plan. They help guide the employer's interests, needs, and requirements, facilitate the plan design, marketing, and implementation process, and often initiate discussions with plans regarding needs or plan maintenance.

3. To market successfully to employers, plans should focus on understanding the general needs of the employer and tailoring value proposition by employer based on the relative important of decision-making criteria.

4. There are seven key needs that drive employer choice.
   - Cost and financial sustainability
   - Compatibility with human resource objectives
   - Network access that is appropriate to the employee population
   - Assurance of quality care
   - Choice among different plan designs
   - Excellent local service
   - A strong partner in health care coverage

5. Today's consumers play a greater role in decision-making partly because they are more self-reliant, better educated, and more affluent than in previous decades. Consumers tend to choose based on six key criteria:
   - Convenient access to quality health care services
   - Appropriate choices of plans
   - Seeing their physician as a resource and they health plan as administrator
   - Low out-of-pocket expenses
   - Easy-to-complete paperwork and little of it
   - Fast and easy access to accurate service and information

6. To consumers, providers represent the MCO and are therefore integral in shaping consumers' satisfaction with their health care; therefore, MCOs should work to negotiate win-win contract situations and maintain effective network management.

7. There is a complex process associated with the sale of managed care services. The marketing and sales departments must work closely throughout this process to ensure the provision of critical information and strategic support.

8. The major steps in the sales process are:
   - *Targeting opportunities*: The department must identify potential new clients.
   - *Prospecting*: In this step, the MCO contacts the targeted employer to communicate the desire to establish a relationship.
   - *Identifying and analyzing needs*: The sales force meets with the prospects to identify the organizations' needs.

- *Underwriting the risk*: The sales force submits key information to the underwriting and other departments and collaborates with underwriting to ensures that any proposal optimizes the MCO's financial performance.
- *Preparing the proposal*: The sales force gathers the information about the company and creates an approach tailored to the needs of the specific employer.
- *Presenting the solution*: The sales force makes a formal presentation of their final proposal showing how the MCO can address their needs.
- *Closing the account*: The sales force seeks a binding commitment from the employer.
- *Consumer sales*: The MCO contacts the employee population for the purpose of advertising and answering specific questions among the employee population.

9. MCOs use television, radio, and print advertising to disseminate information about their products.

10. The sales, marketing, and service departments and the health plan (including health plan staff, network physicians and hospitals, and ancillary service providers) must all work together to supply consumers with the managed care product.

11. Sales and marketing professionals within MCOs must not only work to identify the product and market opportunities and acquire business, but also maintain and manage existing employer relationships and expand them where possible.

CHAPTER 24

The Employer's View of Managed Health Care: Show Me the Value

CHAPTER STUDY REVIEW

1. Managed care trends affect stakeholders—consumers, providers, employers, health plans, and the government—in a variety of ways. Some of the main trends affecting these groups include restructuring, increased competition within health care markets and across industry sectors, the prevalence of consumerism, increasing costs, and a renewed focus on defining and measuring quality.

2. Market trends affect large and small employers in different ways. Large groups are losing leverage with large multisite health plans. Moderate groups are witnessing a reduction in benefits staffing and are also losing leverage. Medium groups are still significantly price sensitive and this will increasingly come into play as costs continue to increase. Small groups are the most price sensitive and will also be affected by continued price increases. They are beginning to migrate away from indemnity-type plans to PPOs and HMOs. Although more small groups are likely to offer some form of health coverage, fewer employees are likely to enroll.

3. Value is an organic concept in the health care field and its definition continues to evolve into the new century. Many MCOs implemented interventions, such as the use of carve-outs for behavioral health care and pharmacy benefit administration, to affect value. However, as the pressures of the late 1980s return (cost increases, deteriorating customer service, increased political intervention), these interventions will no longer provide solutions. Employers now rely on a number of interventions working together to affect value.

4. Today's definition of value is driven by an increased understanding of the impact of employee reward systems on business results. The definition includes the impact of health care delivery on people and

business drivers within their business. In addition, employers are examining the overall alignment of health care delivery with their business strategies.

5. There are eight main trends likely to figure largely in the future of managed health care:
   - Consumerism and technology will remain dominant themes in health care
   - Individual employees with take more responsibility for their health
   - Individual employees and employers will insist on increased accountability for service and quality
   - Competition among plans will continue to increase
   - The involvement of the Internet in health care will continue to increase
   - Medical practice could become systematized and evidence-based through the use of tools and technology
   - The role of employers in providing health benefits for employees will change
   - There will be a change in federal tax laws

CHAPTER 25

The Impact of Consumerism on Managed Health Care

CHAPTER STUDY REVIEW

1. Consumerism in health care is driven by several factors:
   - The overall *growth of consumerism* in society
   - *Employers*, who demand greater value from payers while forcing employees to become more involved on financial and intellectual bases
   - *Government purchasers*, who view consumerism as a rationale for addressing the public's concerns about managed care in addition to problems with health care coverage and costs in the United States
   - *Private accreditation and advocacy groups*, which include the NCQA
   - *Media*, which influences *public perception* by publicizing negative stories about MCOs
   - An increase in *information technology*, which offers increased access to health care information
   - Societal trends such as the spread of anti-institutional sentiment, which leads consumers to question authority, and value placed on self-reliance, which means that patients expect to take responsibility for their own health and health care
2. Overall, today's health care consumers are more educated, demanding, informed, time-constrained, choice hungry, responsive, and clear about their demands.
3. Increased consumerism will require that MCOs engage in several key practices such as:
   - Disseminating meaningful and understandable information on managed care and quality
   - Developing innovative products and services that will satisfy consumers' preferences for choice, convenience, and access

- Support and encourage consumer empowerment in treatment decisions
- Streamline administrative functions to keep costs in lines and prices competitive

4. To keep pace with increased consumerism, MCOs should develop and maintain various avenues for disseminating and filtering information for consumers. They must strive to satisfy consumer demand for innovative products and services, empowerment in treatment decisions, and efficient and streamlined administrative functions.

5. There are four basic elements in the process of developing consumer strategies.
   - Understand how consumerism is developing in the local market
   - Examine industries beyond health care that have a track record for redefining their business operations around the consumer
   - Develop initiatives to support the consumer strategy that are not only effective in the local market, but also leverage the organization's current capabilities, resources, and infrastructure
   - Develop initiatives to support the strategy that reflect a broad range of investments regarding scale and scope of resources and time frame for development and implementation

CHAPTER 26

Accreditation and Performance Measurement Programs for Managed Care Organizations

CHAPTER STUDY REVIEW

1. Approximately half of the country's HMO and POS plans participate in some kind of accreditation program. Though accreditation is not mandatory in all states, many employers will not contract with a plan unless it has earned some form of external accreditation.

2. The NCQA is an independent group that accredits HMO and POS plans. Review teams consist of one to two administrative and three or four physician reviewers. These teams review plans in the areas of quality management and improvement, utilization management, credentialing, member rights and responsibilities, preventive health services, medical records, and HEDIS performance.

3. NCQA reports indicate plan performance in five categories: access and service, qualified providers, staying healthy, getting better, and living with illness.

4. Beyond HMO and POS plans, NCQA sponsors several additional certification and accreditation programs including those for managed behavioral healthcare organizations, PPOs, CVOs, new health plans that would not otherwise qualify for NCQA accreditation participation, and physician organization certification.

5. HEDIS is a set of standardized measures that examine plan performance across a variety of areas. HEDIS specifies not only what to measure, but how to measure it. The areas covered by HEDIS are:
   - Effectiveness of care
   - Access to or availability of care
   - Member satisfaction
   - Use of services

- Cost of care
- Informed health care choices
- Health plan descriptive information

6. The Utilization Review Accreditation Commission (URAC) was founded in response to the concerns and frustration with the diversity of UR procedures and the growing impact of UR on physicians and hospitals. URAC's UM standards can be applied to stand-alone UM organizations or to UM functions that are integrated into health benefits programs.

7. URAC standards cover six main categories:
   - Confidentiality
   - Staff qualifications
   - Program qualifications
   - Accessibility
   - UM information
   - Review determination

8. URAC also offers both PPO and HMO accreditation programs that assess standards in four areas—network management standards, provider credentialing, member protection, and quality management.

9. The Joint Commission evaluates and accredits hospitals and other health care organizations. The Joint Commission accredits MCOs under its network accreditation program and the standards cover eight areas:
   - Rights, responsibilities, and ethics
   - Continuum of care
   - Education and communication
   - Health promotion and disease prevention
   - Network leadership
   - Human resources management
   - Information management
   - Network performance improvement

10. After an organization is surveyed by the Joint Commission, it is placed in one of six categories—accreditation with commendation, accreditation, accreditation with recommendations for improvement, conditional accreditation, preliminary nonaccreditation, and not accredited. Results of Joint Commission surveys are then made available online.

CHAPTER 27

Common Operational Problems in Managed Health Care Plans

CHAPTER STUDY REVIEW

1. There are many operational problems common to MCOs. Often, the identification and resolution of one problem can lead to the discovery of additional problems within the health plan.

2. *Undercapitalization*, a problem common especially for start-ups, can result from the quick accrual of losses due to high start-ups costs or low pricing strategy. Later on, it can result from sustained operating losses or an acquisition that results in a large loss in capital.

3. *Unrealistic projections* are common in new plans. They often include the overprojection of enrollment and underprojection of medical expenses.

4. A problem often found in start-up plans is predatory pricing (low-balling). In this situation, premium rates are set intentionally well below the actual cost of delivering care. This can lead to a continuing loss situation.

5. *Overpricing* is a problem usually found in mature plans, but can also occur in newer plans. Overpricing occurs when rates in the market-place are unacceptably high.

6. *Uncontrolled growth* can be caused by many factors such as a hot market, products and prices that are highly competitive, the acquisition of a competing health plan, and the failure of a competitor. Though plan growth is good, uncontrolled growth can outstrip the plan's capabilities.

7. The *failure to manage a reduction in growth* can cause a rapid rise in the medical loss ratio and strain the ability of the plan to support administrative costs.

8. Lower premium yields, lower growth, and adverse selection can result from a *failure to use underwriting*. It can have many causes including neglect of the proper underwriting guidelines, lack of communication between a salesperson and an underwriter, and a failure to approach rate setting in the context of the market.

9. *Adverse selection* can be caused by the enrollment of members who have higher medical needs than those enrolled in other plans, the addition of new members who have higher medical needs than average, or the loss of existing members whose medical needs are lower than average. Adverse selection can cause an increase in premium rates and can even send plans into an "insurance death spiral" in which premium hikes never catch up with medical costs, but do result in continually losing membership so that the only remaining members have unsupportably high medical expenses.

10. Rapid growth or failure to accrue properly for expenses that are incurred but not reported can cause *a severe insufficiency in financial reserves for medical expenses*.

11. Another common operational problem is the failure to reconcile accounts receivable and membership, which can result from a lack of an accurate and regular membership reconciliation function. The result is the need for a substantial write-down of revenues.

12. Organizations with *overextended management* often have a diminished ability to change and adapt to the competitive environment and subordinates and providers may suffer demoralization. This problem is often caused by rapid growth and a failure to keep up with changing management requirements, as well as the hiring of managers with improper skills.

13. Inaccurate forecasting and budgeting and the production of an excess of reports can result from a *failure of management to produce or understand reports*.

14. There are many potential causes for the *failure to track correctly medical cost and utilization*. Growing plans may develop problems with their systems, expenses may be allocated improperly, there may be problems with claims processing, authorization systems may be loose, the medical director may fail to understand the numbers, or utilization may be tracked improperly.

15. A failure of MIS to keep pace with plan growth, the use of legacy systems of an acquired plan, and a failure to keep up with e-commerce and the Internet may cause *systems inability to manage the business*.

16. *Failure to educate and reeducate providers* can cause the improper use of the system by both providers and office staff.

17. Some plans suffer from their *failure to deal with difficult or noncompliant providers*. The plan may then have to absorb the

expenses of the physician's utilization of resources, the physician may transmit his or her negative attitude to plan members, and the physician's attitude and behavior may promote poor attitudes among the plan's physicians and staff.

18. A final operational problem common to many MCOs is *hubris*. This often occurs when plan managers believe their own good press, when managers refuse to heed danger signs, and when pride of accomplishment prevents managers from seeing things as they are in actuality.

CHAPTER 28

Operational Finance and Budgeting

CHAPTER STUDY REVIEW

1. An MCO's product pricing strategies form the basis of its overall financial management. After the establishment of pricing strategies, an MCO develops a detailed operating budget.

2. Though MCOs are regulated primarily at the state level, some federal regulations may be imposed when an MCO offers a federally regulated product such as Medicare risk contracts. MCOs that are held publicly are subject to the rules and regulations of the SEC. Two state-based organizations that have an interest in MCO function are the Department of Insurance and the Department of Health.

3. Financial managers must address the many and varied interests of a variety of people including senior managers, insurance regulators, the SEC, tax authorities, and investors.

4. Financial statements have five key components:
   - *Operating statement*: This is a high-level profit and loss statement.
   - *Premium revenue*: This is the primary revenue source for HMOs. Premiums are generally received in advance for coverage of a month-long period.
   - *Other revenue sources*: These can include fee revenue from PPO members, coordination of benefits recoverable, reinsurance recoverable, and interest income.
   - *Medical expenses*: This covers physician, hospital, and ancillary services and expenses may be incurred on a capitated basis, fee schedule, or per diem arrangement.
   - *Administrative expenses*: These include salaries and sales, marketing, and other operating expenses.

5. A balance sheet includes seven basic elements:
   - *Cash and investments*: This represents a significant portion of the balance sheet for an HMO.

- *Premium receivable*: Premiums are usually collected monthly.
- *Other assets*: A typical large asset may be fixed assets.
- *Unearned premiums*: These are premiums received by the MCO at the close of the financial reporting period that have not been earned, usually because they have been paid in advance.
- *Claims payable and IBNR*: The basis for recording claim reserves depends on information provided by other operating areas of the MCO.
- *Risk pool liabilities*: Reimbursement strategies may involve risk pools. In these instances, MCOs must maintain accurate records of payment withholds from physicians and hospitals.
- *Equity*: MCOs must track both SAP and GAAP basis equity.

6. MCOs are subject to certain regulatory reporting considerations. Depending on the type of plan, an MCO will have to submit quarterly financial statements, annual statements, Schedules D and L, certification on claims reserves, and audited financial statements.

7. Financial forecasts predict activity and results beyond the current period and are important tools for financial management. They are often developed up several months in advance of the reporting period and in generating them, the financial manager seeks a balance between simplicity of a summary level and complexity of actual details required.

CHAPTER 29

Underwriting and Rating Functions Common to Most Markets

CHAPTER STUDY REVIEW

1. Ideally, underwriting and rating create a balance among factors such as adequacy, competitiveness, and equity of rates.
   - *Adequate rates* are high enough to generate sufficient revenue to cover plan expenses and yield an acceptable rate of return on equity.
   - *Competitive rates* are low enough to sell cases and enroll enough members to meet growth targets.
   - *Equitable rates* approximate a group's costs with a reasonable amount of cross-subsidization among groups.
2. When effective, underwriting focuses on four areas—individual or group applicants' health status, ability to pay the premium, other coverage (if applicable), and historical persistency.
3. Rating centers on calculating the premium to be charged for a specific individual or group. This calculation is based on information obtained through underwriting and the premium calculation is most often done using a rate formula. The resulting rate is often called the book or manual rate.
4. Three requirements for the rate formula are that they should recognize all health plan costs, be easy to apply in the majority of situations, and result in a premium rate. Rates are typically expressed on a per member per month (PMPM) basis.
5. The majority of rate formulas begin with a base rate—a PMPM incurred medical cost. Projection period base rates are developed through analysis of historical incurred medical costs for a certain time period and a projection forward to the projection period recognizing actual and anticipated changes in the block of business.

6. Incurred claims—calculated through the conversion of paid claim data—are matched with health plan exposure, measured in member months, to develop a base period PMPM cost.

7. Important factors that predict medical cost differences among individuals or groups should be considered in setting rate formula adjustments, but the adjustments should also be easy to measure and apply.

8. The PMPM can be calculated by combining retention with medical costs and dividing the medical costs by a target loss ratio or adding specific PMPM retention costs.

9. Experience is the best data source for health plans. Lacking experience, most plans refer to published sources or actuarial consulting firms for initial medical cost targets based on relevant data.

10. Rate formulas are updated routinely using data from management reports such as financial gain or loss summaries, incurred claims costs, group-specific information, a development incurred by unreported claims, and membership information. In addition, most financial departments produce accounting reports including income statements, balance sheets, and cash flow reports.

11. Carriers may use several different approaches to calculate group-specific rates, which vary by rate structure and degree of community rating.

CHAPTER 30

Medicare and Managed Care

CHAPTER STUDY REVIEW

1. The 1997 BBA affected the relationship between Medicare and private insurance. It expanded the kinds of options available to Medicare beneficiaries and enacted a number of changes in requirements such as payment, rules of enrollment, and contracting standards.

2. There are several requirements for eligibility to Medicare risk contracts.
   - *State licensure*: According to the BBA, organizations must be licensed by the state as risk-bearing entities. HCFA requires that organizations have state-issued certifications noting that the nature of the licensure or authority to offer risk products is consistent with the requirements for the assumption of risk as a Medicare+Choice organization.
   - Before the *repeal of 50/50*, non-Medicare and non-Medicaid enrollees had to compose at least 50 percent of an organization's enrollment. This has now been phased out.
   - Under BBA policy, there is a *minimum enrollment requirement* that, to have a Medicare+Choice contract, organizations must have at least 5,000 members (1,500 members if the plan operates in a rural area).

3. Under the BBA, provider sponsored organizations (PSOs) that meet specified standards may receive a waiver of the state licensure requirements that apply to other Medicare+Choice organizations.

4. A medical savings account can be combined with a Medicare+Choice high-deductible plan that is responsible for covering the full cost of covered care after the deductible is met. In this instance, a part of the capitation payment that would normally go to the Medicare+Choice group is instead deposited into an account used by the beneficiary to finance medical care costs.

5. The BBA also introduced Medicare POS plans that could be offered by Medicare+Choice organizations. Organizations that offer a POS option are subject to monitoring by HFCA to ensure the satisfaction of requirements such as financial solvency and quality assurance.

6. The BBA requires that, within a plan's service area, benefits and premiums offered must be uniform. This forces the organization to make decisions regarding the plans it offers, as well as the area in which they are made available. Before this, HCFA allowed an organization to vary benefits by county. Finally, a segmented service policy was developed. This policy allows an organization to subdivide a service area under a single contract and provide different benefits within the subarea.

7. Medicare uses an administered pricing mechanism to set rates for Medicare+Choice plans. Early in the preceding year, the rates for each calendar year for each county are published. Individual rates vary by fixed demographic factors that apply across the population and payments are risk adjusted at the individual enrollee level.

8. Under BBA, payment is subject to a variety of provisions that determine the change in levels of payment from year-to year. Before BBA, payment was based on local fee-for-service costs.

9. An important change made by BBA is that payments to Medicare+Choice plans will be adjusted for health status of individual enrollees on a phased-in basis. This methodology is being reviewed as of late 2000 because of the high number of Medicare+Choice risk plans that have dropped out of the program.

10. The BBA also balanced the new role of states by restricting the extent to which states can regulate or tax Medicare+Choice plans and included provisions that preempt state law in the Medicare+Choice program for three areas—benefits, provider participation rules, and coverage determination under Medicare+Choice contracts.

11. All Medicare+Choice organizations must sign a standard contract and must comply with the terms of that contract, state and federal regulations and statutes governing the contract, and other federal laws outlined in the contract.

12. Standard contracts include provisions for administrative requirements, benefit provisions requirements, quality standards, reporting and surveying, and external review. In addition, current legislation provides for a number of consumer and provider protections as well as rules regarding enrollment and marketing.

CHAPTER 31

Medicaid Managed Care

CHAPTER STUDY REVIEW

1. Medicaid was developed as the principal program of health care for low-income people. It was originally patterned after private insurance; however, costs were far above estimates and the plan was challenged by rapid growth and medical care cost inflation.
2. Medicaid enrolls three distinct populations—healthy women and children, older and younger people with chronic illness and disability, and those who are institutionalized.
3. Several problems prompted states to look to managed care models to solve some of the problems endemic to Medicaid. Some of these problems were declining provider participation limited access to primary and preventive care, dependence on inappropriate sites of care, and concern regarding the quality of services that beneficiaries were able to receive.
4. States have had mixed results when making the transition to managed care models for Medicaid. These transitions require a great deal of planning and research, as well as time for preparation and implementation. When planning a Medicaid program, states must examine program models, eligibility, enrollment, and choice options; contract specifications as other functions of buying value, compensation, and rates; and provisions for quality monitoring and oversight.
5. Medicaid managed care has met with success in several areas including access, cost, quality and outcomes, consumer satisfaction and responsiveness, accountability, and devolution.
6. Despite its many successes, Medicaid managed care has also fallen short in several areas. Programs have fallen short or failed to deliver in the areas of evidence of impact, administrative capacity and performance, contracting environment, and the service of special needs groups.
7. Like the whole of managed care, Medicaid managed care faces many challenges, both currently and in the future. Such challenges

include rising premiums, more vocal disgruntled customers, increased mandates and strictures by policymakers, consolidation, market withdrawals, failure of health plans, hostile contracting environments, and rates that vary widely.

8. The future of Medicaid managed care will depend on the development of key long-term issues such as:
   - The role of policy makers
   - The alignment of medical agencies' expectations with the ability to pay
   - The development of sustainable relationships with high-quality managed care plans
   - Meshing the competing aims of mainstreaming beneficiaries while maintaining safety net providers
   - The evaluation of value against rates

CHAPTER 32

Legal Issues in Provider Contracting

CHAPTER STUDY REVIEW

1. Despite the wide variations among provider contracts, there are several issues common to the contracting process.
   - The managed care plan should identify key objectives divided into two categories—those that are essential and those that are highly desirable but not essential.
   - The managed care plan should develop a master schedule that identifies the contracts that must be entered into and renewed.
   - A managed care organization must sometimes develop a letter of intent that defines the basic elements of a contemplated arrangement or transaction between the two parties.
   - The plan should devise a negotiating strategy based on objectives and relative negotiating strength.

2. Despite variations in content, contracts have the same basic structure that includes a title, caption, transition, recitals, definitions, closing or testimonium, and appended documents or exhibits.

3. Clauses, provisions, and key factors common to most contracts include:
   - *Names*: The names of the parties entering into the agreement are set forth in the initial paragraph.
   - *Recitals*: These are a series of statements that describe who the parties are and what they are trying to accomplish.
   - *Table of contents*: This helps readers locate pertinent sections within the contract.
   - *Definitions*: This section serves to simplify the reader's understanding of the contract by providing definitions for complicated terms.
   - *Provider obligations*: The obligations cover provider qualifications and credentialing, provider service, nondiscriminatory requirements, compliance with utilization and quality manage-

ment programs, acceptance of enrollee patients, enrollee complaints, and maintenance and retention of records and confidentiality.

- *Payment*: The payment terms are some of the most important provisions for both providers and managed health care plans. This section covers a number of different payment issues and addresses risk-sharing arrangements, payment and physician-hospital organizations, other-party liability, any other payment-related issues, and hold-harmless and no-balance-billing clauses.

- *Relationship of the parties*: Most contracts state that the managed health care plan and the provider have an independent contractual arrangement.

- *Use of name*: Contracts often limit the ability of either party to use the name of the other by identifying the circumstances in which either party's name may be used.

- *Notification*: The managed health care plan will ensure that it is advised of changes that affect the ability of the provider to meet contractual obligations.

- *Insurance and indemnification*: Insurance provisions may cover both professional liability and general liability coverage. Also common are cross-indemnification provisions.

- *Term, suspension, and termination*: The term section sets forth the term of the contract and of any subsequent contact renewals. Some contracts grant the managed health care plan a right of suspension in which the contract continues, but the provider loses specific rights. Termination provisions cover termination without cause and termination with cause.

- *Flow down clauses and provider subcontracts*: Managed care plans may be obligated to flow down some clauses that are included in the contract between the plan and the payer. If the provider will be subcontracting, the contract should include language to specify whether the plan or the provider will credential subcontracting providers.

- *Declarations*: This section of the contract includes answers to a variety of "what if" questions. Such clauses include force majeure, choice of law provisions, merger clauses, assignment of rights clauses, severability clauses, clauses regarding contract amendments, and clauses regarding the methods through which and to whom notices should be provided.

CHAPTER 33

Legal Liability Related to Medical Management Activities

CHAPTER STUDY REVIEW

1. All managed health care plans must devise and maintain medical management programs pursuant to applicable laws, accreditation standards, and agreements with customers. Failure to do so may expose a plan to increased regulatory oversight, legal liability, or loss of business. In worst-case scenarios, the plan may be ordered to stop doing business or be forced out of business.

2. HMOs are usually required to establish medical management programs pursuant to state HMO licensure laws, establish grievance procedures, and comply with federal HMO statutes. Some customer groups also require that HMOs receive accreditation.

3. HCFA requires that Medicare+Choice plans implement quality assessment and performance improvement programs, contract with approved quality review and improvement organizations, and implement specified grievance procedures.

4. The NAIC Model PPO Act requires that PPOs include mechanisms to control utilization and determine if services are medically necessary.

5. The majority of medical management issues involve the denial of claims for services or a failure to authorize providers to render services to members when these services allegedly were to have been covered under a plan's certificate of coverage.

6. Bad faith actions are based on an allegation that a plan violated an implied duty of good faith and fair dealing through the way in which it conducted its medical management activities.

7. Increasingly, actions allege that plans have been negligent when performing medical management activities. Under definitions of negligence, plans are required to render a level of care that would be

rendered by a reasonably prudent managed care organization in similar circumstances in order to avoid causing foreseeable injuries to plan members. Negligence actions can relate to the design of medical management programs, the selection and supervision of participating providers, the compensation of participating providers, and liability for the negligence of participating providers.

8. Plan counsel and management should take care to evaluate and oversee the operation of the plan's medical management program, the objective being the assurance of achieving the objectives of providing high quality covered services to members in a timely and cost-effective manner without exposing the plan to unnecessary liability. To do this, plans should act with reason and good faith when selecting providers, establish medical management policies, procedures, and criteria, draft contracts and membership materials, make medical management determinations, and resolve disputes with both members and providers.

CHAPTER 34

The Health Insurance Portability and Accountability Act of 1996

CHAPTER STUDY REVIEW

1. HIPAA was a dramatic departure from previous legislation in its provision of federal regulatory standards for private health insurance products sold in both the group and individual markets and for self-insured, employer-sponsored plans. Under HIPAA, states share regulatory power with federal agencies that now have some regulatory authority over private health insurance and group health plans. The Act was the first direct regulation of the business of health insurance by the federal government.

2. In addition to portability and access standards, HIPPA includes tax incentives, antifraud and abuse initiatives, and administrative simplification requirements. The Act also benefits the self-employed by increasing gradually the deductibility of health insurance, providing tax incentives for the purchase of long-term care insurance, and authorizing a demonstration program for tax-preferred medical savings accounts.

3. HIPAA is considered a watershed event because it is the first federal law that subjects all health plans to minimum standards of accessibility to health coverage.

4. HIPAA has helped to balance the regulatory weight by granting additional authority to federal agencies. The Act establishes minimum federal standards and generally permits states to offer more protection for consumers regarding portability and access. HIPAA regulations apply to group health plans, health insurance issuers, and the health benefits they provide.

5. Several nondiscrimination provisions are included in HIPAA. These provisions aim to improve access to health coverage in the group market for people with preexisting medical conditions. The Act provides that no health plans or insurers can establish certain rules for eligibility of enrollees and restricts the use of preexisting condition exclusions. It also prohibits health plans and insurers from requiring anyone to pay a premium or contribution larger than fees charged to a similarly situated person on the basis of a health status factor.

6. HIPAA ensures special enrollment periods during which eligible employees or dependents who did not take initial enrollment opportunities are ensured the right to join the health plan.

7. Among the many provisions for health care coverage included in HIPASA are the portability of insurance for those moving into a group plan from previous coverage, the requirement of group insurers and group health plan sponsors to provide documentation to individuals whose coverage is terminated, and access to insurance coverage for small group employers. In addition, HIPAA requires all insurers who offer health insurance coverage in connection with group health plans to renew coverage or continue it in force at the option of the plan sponsor. All of these provisions are subject to specified exceptions.

8. HIPAA requires that all group health plans notify participants regarding reductions in covered services or benefits within 60 days after the measures are adopted.

9. The Act improves access to health insurance for individuals by guaranteeing coverage for certain eligible persons and guaranteeing the renewability of individual market health insurance policies.

10. Among HIPASA's guaranteed availability provisions are the following:
    - It allows individuals who have maintained continuous coverage and then lost it to obtain coverage in the individual market and gives states a choice of alternatives for establishing this guarantee.
    - It requires individual insurers to offer coverage to eligible individuals with no preexisting condition exclusions.
    - It provides that state programs, to qualify as acceptable alternatives to federal fallback requirements, must give all eligible persons a choice in coverage without imposing preexisting condition exclusions.
    - It allows states to make decisions about whether to adopt the federal fallback standards or propose an acceptable alternative mechanism.

11. HIPAA's administrative simplification provisions aim to reduce the costs and administrative burden of health care by enabling the standardized electronic transmission of many administrative and financial transactions that were previously handled on paper. These

provisions will increase vastly administrative efficiency and reduce costs for the health care industry, though many MCOs are not yet able to exchange data electronically as of 2000. The earliest that any of these provisions will be in force is in 2002. The four primary areas for required compliance under the administrative simplification provisions of HIPAA are:

- Compliance with privacy and security requirements
- Compliance with transaction standards—the ANSI X 12N standards
- Compliance with standardized diagnostic and procedure coding
- Compliance with standardized identifiers for providers, payers, and employers

12. EDI refers to the exchange of data through electronic means rather than by paper or telephone.

CHAPTER 35

State Regulation of Managed Care

CHAPTER STUDY REVIEW

1. At the state level, HMOs are often regulated by more than one agency—by insurance regulators, who manage financial aspects and, in some states, external review, and by health regulators who focus on quality of care issues, utilization patterns, and a provider's ability to offer adequate care. Risk-bearing PPOs are usually regulated by departments of insurance.

2. State oversight applies to many aspects of MCO operation including:

   - *Licensure*: HMOs obtain licenses by applying for a COA and applications are usually processed by the insurance department.

   - *Enrollee information*: The HMO model act requires certain levels of communication with HMO enrollees. Individual and group contract holders are entitled to receive a copy of their contracts and regulators require that they are filed with and approved by the regulatory bodies in charge of reviewing contracts. Enrollees also receive an evidence of coverage document, information about how services can be obtained, a list of health plan providers, and notification regarding discontinued participation by the enrollee's PCP. The PPA model act requires similar disclosure to PPO plan enrollees.

   - *Access to medical services*: Under the HMO Model Act, HMOs are required to ensure the availability and accessibility of medical services. The PPA Model Act requires that plans that offer a PPO option ensure a certain level of access to covered services.

   - *Provider issues*: The HMO Model Act requires that MCOs applying for state licensure provide regulators with copies of provider contract forms and the names and addresses of all contracted providers. It also requires that contracts include a hold-harmless clause that protects enrollees against provider claims in the event of plan insolvency. The NAIC Managed Care Plan Network Adequacy Model Act also includes several provider contract provisions.

- *Reports and rate filings*: HMOs must file several reports including annual reports, schedules of premium rates, and updates to information contained in the original COA.
- *Quality assurance and utilization review*: There are several acts that dictate HMO procedures regarding quality assurance and utilization review. Among them are requirements for an HMO to file a description of its quality assurance program; to have in place an internal system that identifies opportunities for improved care, measures provider performance, ensures a certain level of provider input, and collects and analyzes data on overutilization and underutilization of services; and to have in place written policies and procedures for credentialing all health care professionals.
- *Grievance procedures*: The NAIC Model HMO Act requires that HMOs have written procedures designed to effectively address grievances. These procedures must be approved by the appropriate state agency.
- *External appeals*: Most states have policies giving enrollees the right to appeal some cases involving the denial of coverage to an external review entity.
- *Solvency standards and insolvency protections*: The HMO Model Act establishes specific capital, reserve, and deposit requirements that all HMOs must meet. This is in order to prevent HMO insolvencies and protect consumers and other parties from the effects of insolvencies.
- *Financial examinations and site visits*: Regulators are able to conduct inquiries that examine HMO finances, marketing activities, and QA programs. The examination process may include site visits.
- *HIPAA Implementation*: HIPAA set minimum requirements for health care standards. Many states' requirements exceed those set forward those set by HIPAA.
- *Multisite operations*: MCOs that operate in two or more states must comply with the regulations set forth by each jurisdiction.

3. States have authority to regulate additional MCO products including POS offerings, provider-sponsored organizations, specialty HMOs, utilization review organizations, third-party administrators, and self-funded plans.

4. Many states have any willing provider laws that prohibit MCOs from contracting selectively with a limited group of providers. This

has a significant effect on MCOs because the creation of provider panels is central to basic MCO operations.

5. Many states have legislation that dictate procedures through which enrollees can access specialists. Such legislation includes provisions for direct access, the treatment of specialists as PCPs, standing referrals, and open access products.

6. Many states also have legislation to regulate the use of formularies. Such legislation often requires MCOs to disclose their formularies, have in place and disclose procedures through which, in certain circumstances, members can obtain nonformulary drugs.

7. Additional state regulations may address physician antitrust exemptions, utilization review, emergency care, and clinical mandates.

CHAPTER 36

Managed Care's Regulatory Evolution: Driving Change in the New Century

CHAPTER STUDY REVIEW

1. There are four central issues driving current federal health policy:
   - ***Trust fund solvency for Medicare and Social Security***: It is projected that the Medicare Hospital Insurance (HI) Trust Fund will go bankrupt in 2015. Congress passed the BBA in 1997 in part to reduce the rate of growth in HI expenditures.
   - ***Predicting federal health program outlays***: Congress is faced with the challenge of predicting how much money will be needed to pay for federally funded health care from year to year. Under the current system, the federal government pays health care charges incurred by Medicare beneficiaries. Some advocate switching to a premium support system, in which Medicare beneficiaries would receive a payment from the government towards the purchase of an insurance policy.
   - ***Increasing the number of consumer choices***: An issue of Congressional contention is whether the modernized federal health care programs to make them more like the plans available to workers in the private sector. This would be accomplished by expanding consumer choice and areas of coverage, such as the inclusion of prescription drug coverage.
   - ***Managed Medicare competition***: With the BBA, policy makers created a plan to offer expanded choice to Medicare beneficiaries by creating Medicare+Choice, a plan that strives to adopt traditionally private-sector offerings such as HMOs, PSOs, PPOs, PIs, and MSAs. The BBA also requires that the HCFA develop and provide a variety of customer information to educate Medicare+Choice consumers.

2. Congress has already made adjustments to the BBA through the Balanced Budget Refinement Act; however, it will likely consider ways in which the BBA should be modified to counteract unintentional consequences of the BBA's original payment changes.

3. Another hotly debated issue before Congress is consumer protection measures. Congressional representatives hears increasing complaints from constituents regarding the limitations of managed care. Managed care has raised many concerns and policy makers seek to resolve issues such as the rising costs of medical care, improved quality, access issues, and dissemination of health plan information to consumers; however, much of the legislation regarding health care is held up by partisan debates.

4. Technological advances such as the Internet and e-commerce have created unprecedented levels of access to information. Though this has served to provide customers with increased access to health care information, it has created challenges to securing the privacy and confidentiality of such information.

5. The federal has identified as its number-two law enforcement priority the detection and punishment of health care fraud and abuse activities. Congress has provided additional funding to the OIG for the purpose of hiring new investigative staff.

6. Public opinion will continue to play a large role in shaping health care policies. The level of media coverage given to constituents' complaints regarding health care has fueled the majority of legislative interventions.

EPILOGUE

Managed Health Care at the Millennium

CHAPTER STUDY REVIEW

1. Since the advent of organized health care systems in the United States, there has never been a time these systems have been in stasis. In recent history, these systems have evolved at an extraordinary pace. The complex nature of health systems has made it relatively impossible to predict the ways in which they will evolve.

2. Though it is not possible to say with certainty that the chaos theory applies fully to health care systems, the five central attributes of the theory are relevant to health systems:
   - The object under study is a system that can be described and modeled.
   - The system model contains essential nonlinearity.
   - Vast and numerous complex forces affect the system.
   - Extreme sensitivity to initial conditions exists.
   - Feedback of current conditions affects subsequent results, usually with significant (but not random) variation.

3. Predicting and acting in the chaotic environment of managed health care is difficult, but not impossible. The most that can be done is to understand that the nature of managed health care is that it will change continually. Unfortunately, how it will change cannot be predicted with certainty.

4. There are five elements necessary to think and plan strategically.
   - The presence of a solid and continually refreshing fact base
   - A systematic removal of impeding cultural biases
   - The pace of change undertaken
   - The scenario planning that accounts for time frame, level of risk, and relationship to core mission
   - The metrics and measurements used to track and manage change must be consistent with the strategies and tactics taken

5. There are four basic options available to managers within the complex health care system.

- *Shape the future*: The right action should be taken at the right time. Managers must set new standards that will force the shape of the market. The competition will then be forced to follow.
- *Be a fast follower*: Managers can, with speed, agility, and constant market intelligence, follow quickly on the heels of competitors who make moves to shape the future.
- *Hedge your bets*: This strategy will never create market leaders, but will allow an organization to avoid being left behind. Managers using this tactic make sufficient investments to cover a variety of scenarios and follow through on only those that have low risk and are necessary to remain competitive.
- *Mix the previous options*: Managers may choose to implement a mixture of the previous options to create an overall strategic portfolio.

Notes

<u>Notes</u>

Notes

Notes

Notes

Notes

Notes